STOP
SLAMMING©
THE DOOR
Brien Perry
Illustrations by Blair Webb

Stop Slamming the Door!™

Brien Perry

Published by: Brien Perry Publishing, "It's All Mind",
Sherman Oaks, California
Visit author website at www.BrienPerry.com.

Library of Congress Cataloging-in-Publication Data (in progress)

ISBN-13: 978-0-9980260-4-6

Printed in the United States of America

I'd like to give a special thank you to Karrie Ross.
To my new friend who said YES; which in turn has helped
orchestrate and illuminate the next chapter in my life.
Thank you, Thank you, Thank you!

Book Design and Consulting by www.KarrieRoss.com
Illustrations by Blair Webb

First Edition:

10 9 8 7 6 5 4 3 2 1

Dedicated to

PopPop

May the prettiest of
flowers bloom in your name.

Stop slamming the door you meddlesome four with your friends the onion heads on route to the general store. For lollipops, licorice, gummies and more always forgetting yourselves to stop slamming the door.

LAM!

SLAM!

Stop slamming the door you meddlesome four every summer you slam my candy store door. Running a muck through my candy store tour, stuffing your pockets and bags till they spill to the floor. Just like last summer and the ones all before... “oh please, oh please learn to mature, get a job and stop slamming my door.”

S
494
7953

AM!
STOP SLAMMING THE DOOR!!
Stop slamming the door you meddlesome
four is what POP POP would say as
we took our boards to the shore.
Beating the hinges, shaking the glass and
dropping sand to the floor, “Oh please oh please
my little chickadees, stop slamming the door.”

ME GO TOO

When we were young and fun and lived our lives on the run; we played "FREEDOM" by the nuns till the sun was all done.

SLAM

And as we ran in the house
like elephants from a mouse,
we heard stop slamming the
door you meddlesome four.

SLAM!
SLAM!

SLAM!
SLAM
Since when we were kids from the time we were four, we were always told to stop slamming the door.
SLAM!

For when you slam the
door you create a roar from a
door that was made to keep
you secure.

And if that door ever failed to secure because the meddlesome four kept slamming the door. Wearing out the nails, screws and wood to the core. Letting in the wind, little critters and maybe the screen door tore?

SLAM!
Then POP POP for sure would let out a roar and stop playing his cards and address the loud four.

He said "Hey you four who keep slamming MY door... I've got an idea! No, rather a chore."

"It's an idea I've had and
I don't mean to vent, but
I have an idea and it's a place
you'll be sent."

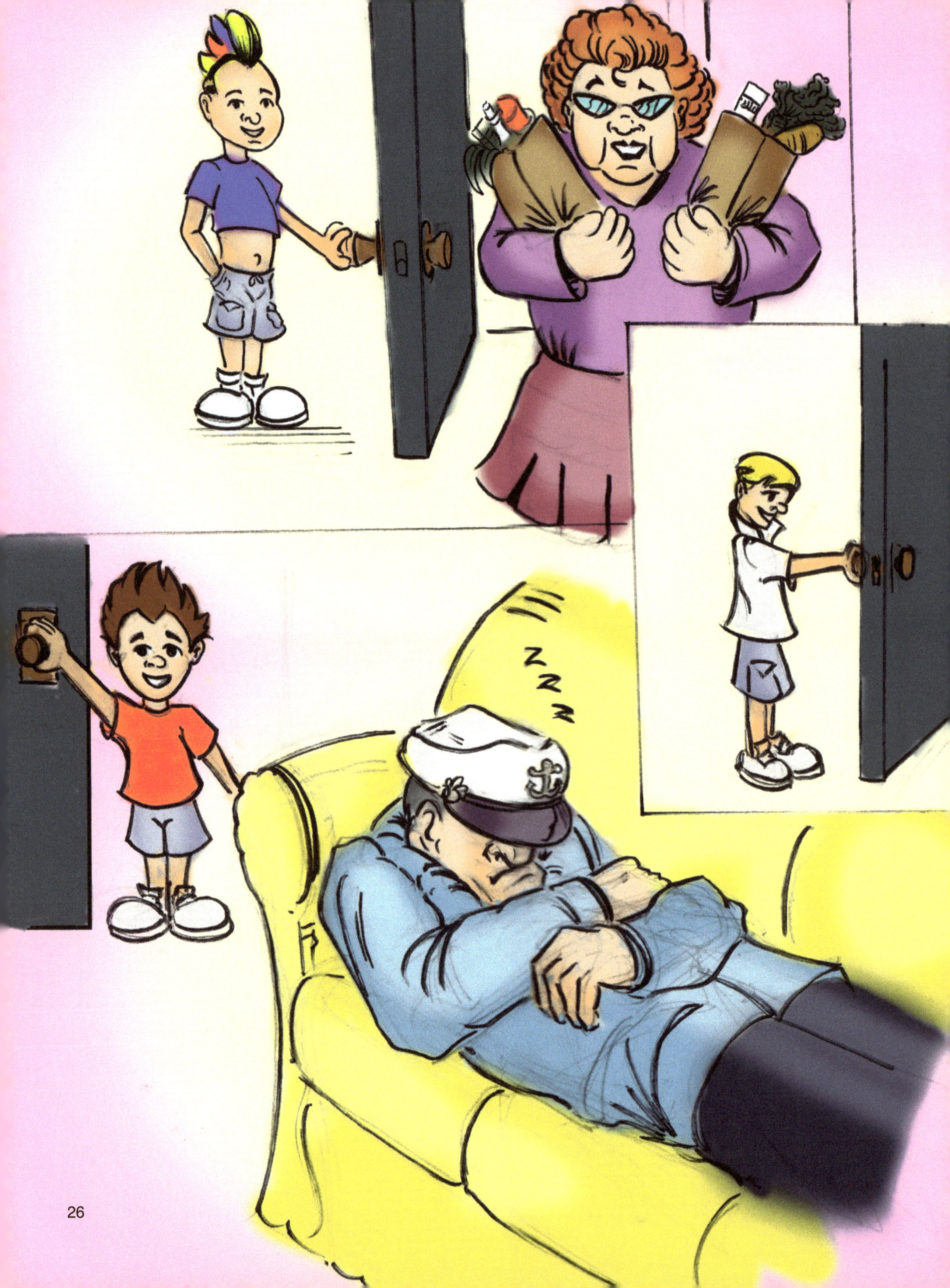
Z
Z
Z

"Because as you get older you're supposed to mature and learn to behave and stop slamming the door."

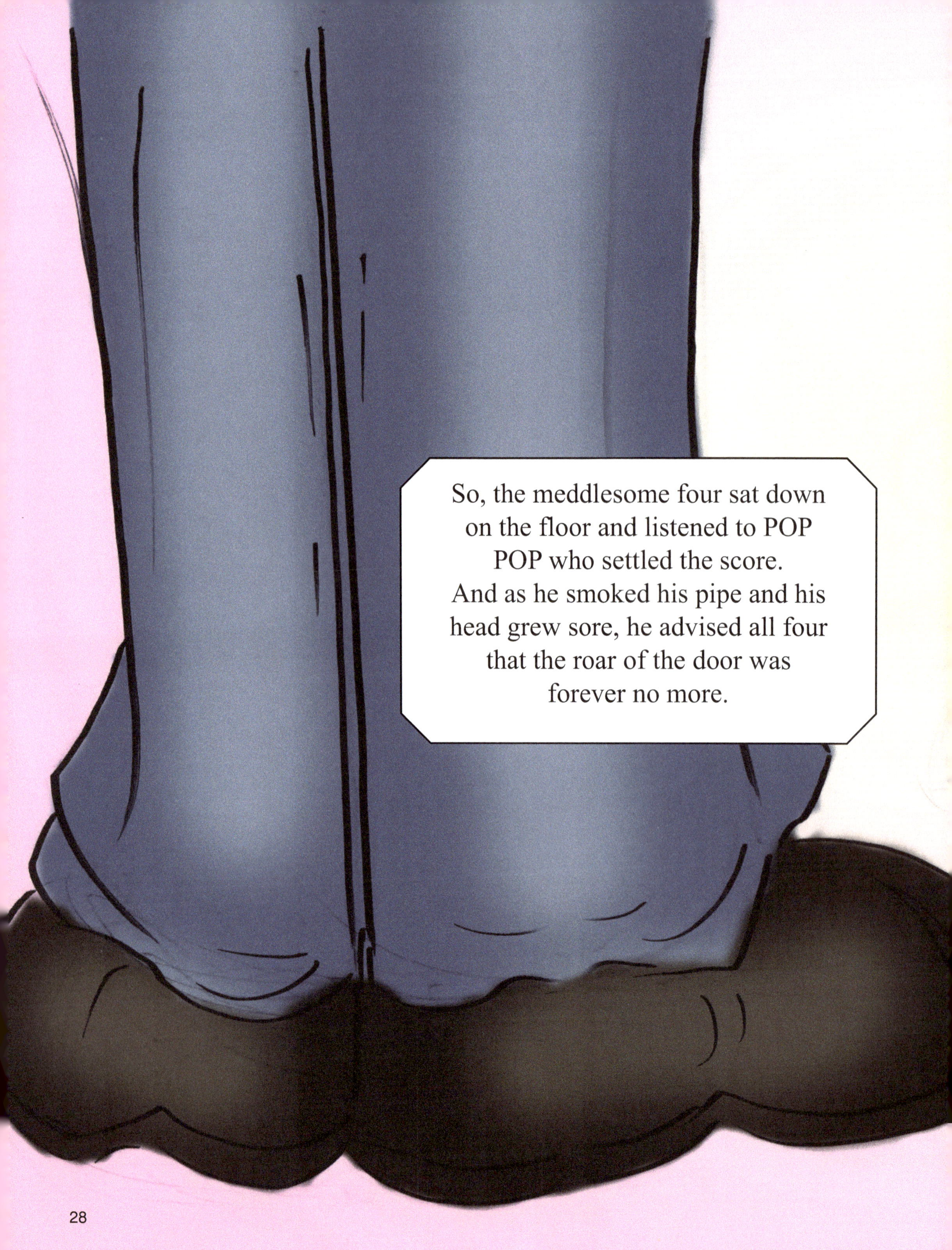

So, the meddlesome four sat down on the floor and listened to POP POP who settled the score. And as he smoked his pipe and his head grew sore, he advised all four that the roar of the door was forever no more.

You are all too young to pay rent!
SO, if that door were to ever slam once more.
You four will all be living outside in a tent.

LOOPER

Then Kevin looked at Kyle, then
Brien to John as the meddlesome
four stopped carrying on.

OOOO

They all realized what was in store and as their mouths quickly opened and dropped to the floor, that meddling core understood for sure how wrong it was to keep slamming the door.

So, from that day forward they all swore that the meddlesome four would stop slamming the door.

And let me tell you my friends, I don't mean to implore, but peace and harmony begin to occur when we all take a pause to reflect and explore how rude it is to keep slamming the door.

ALSO ...
to the shores of LBI...
Thank you for the memories

SLAM!

CPSIA information can be obtained
at www.ICGtesting.com
Printed in the USA
BVHW020228290322
632736BV00021B/253

9 780998 026046